D0627246

To: ....

50¢

From: ....

GLORIA

Children's Books

GLORIA
Children's Books

The Apostles' Creed

"What We Believe"

by Daniel A. Lord, S.J.

The Apostles' Creed
What We Believe

On Sundays and Holy Days,
we pray the Creed.
This is a great Act of Faith.
It was written a long time ago.
It shows that we know the truth.
It says that we have listened
to Jesus Christ.
It means that we believe in
His Church.

4

5

I believe in God,
the Father almighty,
Creator of heaven and earth,
and in Jesus Christ,
His only Son, our Lord,
who was conceived by
the Holy Spirit,
born of the Virgin Mary,
suffered under Pontius Pilate,
was crucified, died and was buried;
He descended into hell;
on the third day He rose again
from the dead;

He ascended into heaven,
and is seated at the right hand of
God the Father almighty;
from there He will come to judge
the living and the dead.
I believe in the Holy Spirit,
the holy catholic Church,
the communion of saints,
the forgiveness of sins,
the resurrection of the body,
and life everlasting. Amen.

We call it the Apostles' Creed.
Many believe that the Apostles
themselves wrote it.
They were the dear friends of Jesus
and His messengers.
He taught them,
and they teach the world.
but we all know that this is
what they believed.
Here is the Good News that Jesus
came to teach the world.
Here are the truths that will make us
happy forever.

I believe ...

This is our great act
of faith. Jesus came to teach us about
God and how to reach Heaven.
He loved us and wanted us
to live forever.
So what He taught us was taught to
us by our best friend.
He was also the wisest of men and
the divine Son of God.
He said to His Apostles, "Go out and
teach all nations."
And, "He that hears you,
hears me."
So I believe Jesus. And I believe the
Apostles, whom He sent.

12

ST. PETRUS ET ST. PAULUS

13

I believe in God ...

I believe that He is my dear
and Heavenly Father.
Long, long ago He created the earth.
He has all power; He used that
power to make the world.
He set the sun, the stars, and the
moon in the sky.
He filled the land with good and
beautiful things.
And then He made for me a lovely
mansion in Heaven.
If I am good on earth, I shall be
happy in Heaven.

15

I believe ... in Jesus Christ, His only Son, Our Lord ...

The Second Person of the Blessed
Trinity came to earth.
He was conceived by the Holy Spirit.
Mary was His lovely Mother.
Because He was born in Bethlehem,
we have Christmas Day.
He taught us all truth;
He did nothing but good for all.
He said, "I am the way and the truth,
and the life."

He suffered under Pontius Pilate ...
He is my Savior, my Master, my Lord,
and my God.
I believe that He suffered
and died for me.
How good and generous Jesus was!
He took upon Himself the sins of all
the world, my sins too.
He was condemend by the Roman
governor, Pontius Pilate.

19

*He was crucified died
and was buried ...*
He died on the Cross for my sins and
the sins of all mankind.
He suffered the Passion so that we
could be forgiven by God.
And when He died, He went down
into limbo and freed the souls
imprisoned there.

He rose from the dead ...

What a wonderful day Easter is!
I believe that on that happy day
Jesus rose from the dead.
Never again would He die; never
again would He suffer.
And because He rose,
I shall rise someday. I shall live forever.
Then on Ascension Thursday,
He went up into Heaven.
He sits upon a beautiful Throne,
asking mercy and grace for us.
And when we die, He will come to judge us.
If we are good, we shall enter into
eternal happiness with Him.

23

I believe in the Holy Spirit ...
This is the Third Person of the
Blessed Trinity.
Jesus promised that He would come
and be our friend.
He would teach us all truth.
He would light our ways.
He would be our strength
and give us grace.
So He came to the Apostles on the
feast of Pentecost.
He comes to me in Confirmation.

24

I believe in the holy Catholic Church...

I believe all that it teaches.
It is the Church of Jesus Christ.
It is the Church of the Apostles.
So I believe that it exists on earth,
in Heaven, and in purgatory.
I believe that my sins
can be forgiven if I'm sorry.
I believe that if I am good
I shall live forever.
Amen.

27